Love Thy Self

Laquinta Horton

BookLeaf Publishing

India | USA | UK

Presentation by *BookLeaf Publishing*

Web: www.bookleafpub.com

E-mail: info@bookleafpub.com

ISBN: 9789363306547

First edition 2024

My Kindness Is My Strength

In all your attempts to humble me, it is evident that my presence is one of reckoning—a light illuminating all your faults. I can hear the progression of your negative chatter. Blind by the eyes of an envious admirer. My success inspired a rage in pursuit of proving that you were better than I. Despite your mediocre efforts to hide your malicious intentions, the goddess in me laughed and graced you with the very thing you lack: decency.

I Am More Than My Circumstances

No one ever thinks about the consequences of dysfunction. The impact it has on the lives of many. Its trauma is bonded to the souls of those who try to escape it, sentencing them to an eternal fight or flight. It forces one to choose their own moral compass in the face of generational disruption. Ignoring what it means for the future to be unknowing of its past. One runs when confronted with the causation of its stifled nature.

Allowing what goes on in the house of the oppressed to linger and stay. One must find the willingness to thrive and the courage to stand against those who felt it was ok to repeat the same crimes.

My Hair Is Beauty

I love the way my strands curl, bending and twisting like acrobatic strings in a symphony.

When I look in the mirror, I see beautiful clouds—thick and soft like pillows. My hair warms my head at just the right temperature. Sitting pretty and still on my crown. It radiates in the sunlight and grows upright toward the sky, resembling the image of trees in nature. My hair defies gravity encrypted with the DNA of the ether—audacious and rare. My hair uniquely stands out amongst all those who stare.

I Am Life

Simplicity, a treasure unnoticed. Hidden by the intricacies of our made-up world. We lost ourselves in the show-and-tell. Too cowardly to admit that we were at our best when we had less. Robbing ourselves of authenticity. We look for the same stars who made us who we are. Searching for above and below like they're separate entities. Not knowing our vessels were the imitation of galaxies.

I Am Resilience

5

I mourned the sins I did not commit, making myself feel guilty for the atrocities committed against me. I purged them of their treachery and made them innocent to all the ears that would listen to me. Giving my heart to the enemy to prove to those who stood against me that I could make a throne impenetrable to attacks. I gave the traitors the keys to the kingdom where my spectators would watch, only to find myself cornered in a tower with a sword that couldn't pierce my heart.

I Vow to Forgive

You could never make me hate you. Even through your lies and deception, my love for you remains strong despite your distasteful actions.

My Essence Is Unrivaled

Your smile. Your heart. Triggered their insecurities. Deep down they knew they couldn't compete with your divinity.

Alchemy Is at My Will

I owe it to myself to win. I owe it to myself to open the doors of opportunity with or without your lending hand. I owe it to myself to walk in the shoes of my predecessors and not question who I am. I own the right to wear my stripes with no explanation. I own the right to walk the streets and not beg for your protection. I own the right to be myself and not ask for your acceptance. I deserve the right to be credited without justifying my successes.

My Love Is the Only Love I Need

Don't be too quick to give away your affections. Handing out your love to things unknowing of your essence. Hold steadfast to your truth; all you need is within you. There is no external gratification. Or a love greater than your own. Love with wisdom. Love with passion. Love yourself more and you'll thank yourself after.

I Am Worthy of Unconditional Love

They say that eyes are the portal to one's soul, revealing the secrets of hidden motives when mouths are closed. It's funny how they look at you when you're young and fresh. Your presence brings them joy and they compete amongst each other to see who loves you the best. But as youth leaves and you become mature, the eyes that once gleamed at your sight turn dark and envious green overnight. Never giving out warning or precaution. Their love for you falters. The veil of youth shatters, removing the protective covering over your sacred eyes. You grow to learn that it's better to love yourself without conditions than to chase love's disguise.

Rejection Is Protection

I was hurt and angry that you didn't choose me. I was upset that you gave another woman everything you said you'd give me. I was furious when I remembered the day you asked me how you should propose. I was livid when I saw that pregnancy picture on your post. Then, I remembered: my creator told me that rejection is protection. Even though my heart was sunken, I knew that you and I weren't destined. I knew that even though you pretended to be a nice guy, you suffered from nothing but a guilty conscience because you told so many lies. I knew you couldn't handle a woman so liberated, so unique. You had to settle for someone foolish enough to put up with your deceit. So, congratulations Mr. & Mrs. C. I would hate to be you, because the love you have couldn't compete with the love that resides in me.

I Will Not Give in to Fictitious Love

I fell in love with the idea of loving another person, because they made it look so easy. They made it look like I could walk on water and survive. But fairytales don't always factor in reality. They never tell you about the sacrifices you have to make just to make another person happy. Or how much of yourself you have to give to live in a state of harmony. They just promoted a story that gave you hope without ever considering the true cost of combining souls. If I had a time machine, I would tell my younger self to look within. I would tell myself not to believe in everything with glitz and glam.

I Am a Beautiful Phenomenon

I love the way I make you mad. The way I stand firm in my beliefs. The way I challenge your authority and your misguided acts. I am a reminder that simple minds never get far in a world of tangible things. You get mad at my deviance, because you can't see past your programmer's dreams. I'm the one hair that never lays flat on your head. I point in the direction of the sky, because I don't mind facing something different from my central point of vision. I love being the anomaly in your perfectly congruent dataset. I change the way you view your reality. I breathe life into impossibility.

I Love the Skin I Am in

I love the way the pigment hugs our skin. The way it colors us in with different tints. The way it sparkles in a sun-kissed bliss. The way it commands attention and leads strangers astray. I love our skin. The one we must protect. The one we must defend. The one that adds character to the monotonous blend. Our skin is not a trend—it is not there for your entertainment; it is not there for your cosplay. It was created to diversify the world and bring life into the canvas.

The Power Is Within Me

Growing is realizing the power you have to dictate their actions. The power you have to deny their pleasures. The strength you have to uphold your standards. The ability you have to control who enters.

I Am the Manifestation of Love

If I count the times I blinded my eyes, it would be close to ten. Daydreaming about the day I'll have that fairytale ending. I became a fool in love with the idea of made-up films, letting the delusions play freely in my head. I thought the love I imagined was fictitious, not realizing the power of creation. I didn't recognize the presence of love I was generating inside.

I Am the Soul of Creation

Let me be the light in the dark. The heat in the cold. The beat to your heart. The key to your soul. Let me be the air for your breath. The cure to your wound. The shield from the storm. The healer I was born. Let me be a womb to the man. A creation of life existing infinitely in my hands.

I Am the Revelation of Love

In a realm where energies intertwine, I found a love within myself—so profound, a cosmic sign. My thoughts dance into the abyss as my heart finds a home in the sacred space of my soul. I let the emotional spirits runneth over in the haven of the creator's throne.